CONTINENTS

SOUTH AMERICA

Ewan McLeish

WAYLAND

CONTINENTS

AFRICA

ANTARCTICA

ASIA

AUSTRALIA AND
OCEANIA

EUROPE

NORTH AMERICA

SOUTH AMERICA

First published in 1996 by
Wayland (Publishers) Limited
61 Western Road, Hove
East Sussex, BN3 1JD, England
© Copyright 1996 Wayland (Publishers) Limited

Picture acknowledgements: Camera Press 17 (bottom); Eye
Ubiquitous 39; Robert Harding 20, 41 (bottom); John Hillelson
Agency 19; Hutchison Library 8, 15, 21 (top), 26; Panos 25 (both),
30, 33 (top), 35, 42 (both); Edward Parker 17 (top), 29, 43; South
American Pictures 24, 33 (bottom), 37; Frank Spooner 13; Still
Pictures 28; Tony Stone 9, 11 (both), 21 (middle), 21 (bottom), 22,
23, 31 both, 34, 36, 38, 40, 41 (top); Sygma 18, 27; Trip 16.

Produced for Wayland (Publishers) Limited
by *specialist* publishing services, London
Designer: Mark Whitchurch

British Library Cataloguing in Publication Data
McLeish, Ewan
    South America. - (Continents)
    1. South America - Juvenile literature
    I. Title
    980' .039

ISBN 0750216204

Typeset by Mark Whitchurch Art & Design, England
Maps by Peter Bull
Graph artwork by Mark Whitchurch
Printed and bound in Italy by G. Canale

CONTENTS

SOUTH AMERICA BY COUNTRY

NORTHERN SOUTH AMERICA

Northern South America is a patchwork of smaller countries and native (indigenous) languages. The countries of the north-east coast still show the influence of European nations like Britain, France and The Netherlands, who established colonies in the seventeenth century.

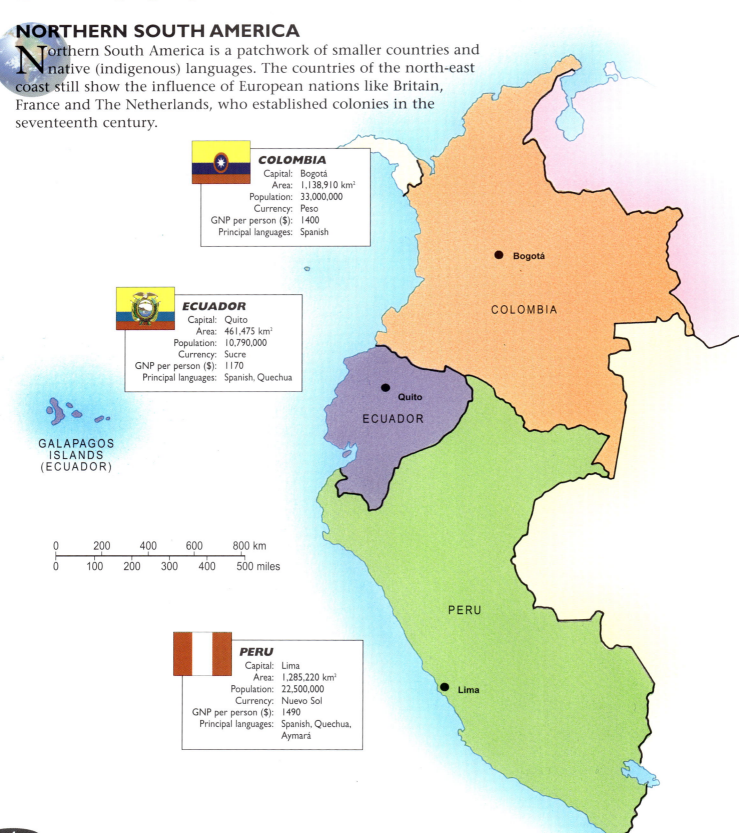

COLOMBIA
Capital: Bogotá
Area: 1,138,910 km²
Population: 33,000,000
Currency: Peso
GNP per person ($): 1400
Principal languages: Spanish

ECUADOR
Capital: Quito
Area: 461,475 km²
Population: 10,790,000
Currency: Sucre
GNP per person ($): 1170
Principal languages: Spanish, Quechua

GALAPAGOS
ISLANDS
(ECUADOR)

0   200   400   600   800 km
0 100 200 300 400 500 miles

Bogotá

COLOMBIA

Quito

ECUADOR

PERU

Lima

PERU
Capital: Lima
Area: 1,285,220 km²
Population: 22,500,000
Currency: Nuevo Sol
GNP per person ($): 1490
Principal languages: Spanish, Quechua,
Aymará

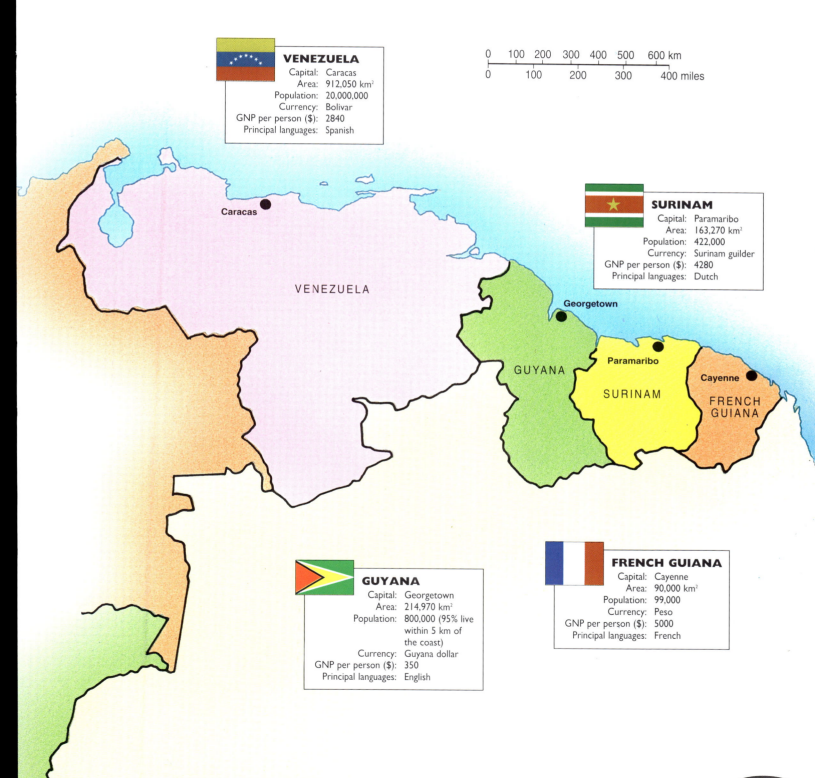

VENEZUELA

Capital:	Caracas
Area:	912,050 km²
Population:	20,000,000
Currency:	Bolivar
GNP per person ($):	2840
Principal languages:	Spanish

0   100   200   300   400   500   600 km
0   100   200   300   400 miles

SURINAM

Capital:	Paramaribo
Area:	163,270 km²
Population:	422,000
Currency:	Surinam guilder
GNP per person ($):	4280
Principal languages:	Dutch

Caracas

Georgetown

VENEZUELA

GUYANA

Paramaribo

Cayenne

SURINAM

FRENCH GUIANA

GUYANA

Capital:	Georgetown
Area:	214,970 km²
Population:	800,000 (95% live within 5 km of the coast)
Currency:	Guyana dollar
GNP per person ($):	350
Principal languages:	English

FRENCH GUIANA

Capital:	Cayenne
Area:	90,000 km²
Population:	99,000
Currency:	Peso
GNP per person ($):	5000
Principal languages:	French

CENTRAL AND SOUTHERN SOUTH AMERICA

Central and Southern South America is dominated by huge countries, like Brazil and Argentina. Much of its culture and architecture show the strong influence of Spanish and Portuguese during the sixteenth century.

| 0 | 200 | 400 | 600 | 800 | 1000 km |
| 0 | 100 | 200 | 300 | 400 | 500 | 600 miles |

BRAZIL

• Brasilia

• La Paz

BOLIVIA

PARAGUAY

Asuncion

BOLIVIA
Capital: La Paz
Area: 1,098,580 km²
Population: 7,400,000
Currency: Boliviano
GNP per person ($): 770
Principal languages: Spanish, Quechua, Aymará

BRAZIL
Capital: Brasilia
Area: 8,511,970 km²
Population: 154,300,000
Currency: Cruzeiro
GNP per person ($): 3020
Principal languages: Portuguese

PARAGUAY
Capital: Asuncion
Area: 406,750 km²
Population: 4,500,000
Currency: Guarani
GNP per person ($): 1500
Principal languages: Spanish, Guaraní

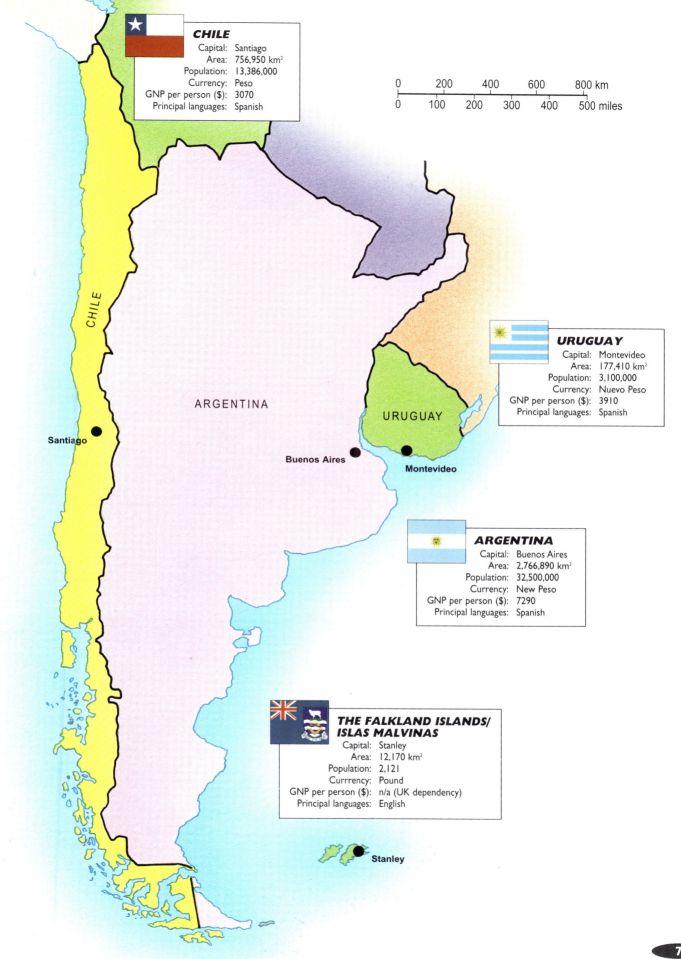

CHILE
Capital: Santiago
Area: 756,950 km²
Population: 13,386,000
Currency: Peso
GNP per person ($): 3070
Principal languages: Spanish

0   200   400   600   800 km
0 100 200 300 400 500 miles

CHILE

ARGENTINA

Santiago

Buenos Aires

URUGUAY
Capital: Montevideo
Area: 177,410 km²
Population: 3,100,000
Currency: Nuevo Peso
GNP per person ($): 3910
Principal languages: Spanish

URUGUAY

Montevideo

ARGENTINA
Capital: Buenos Aires
Area: 2,766,890 km²
Population: 32,500,000
Currency: New Peso
GNP per person ($): 7290
Principal languages: Spanish

THE FALKLAND ISLANDS/
ISLAS MALVINAS
Capital: Stanley
Area: 12,170 km²
Population: 2,121
Currrency: Pound
GNP per person ($): n/a (UK dependency)
Principal languages: English

Stanley

INTRODUCTION

In 1498 the Genoese explorer Christopher Columbus, sailing under a Spanish flag, sighted the coast of South America. Columbus thought this 'new world' was part of Asia, but 2 years later the Italian explorer, Amerigo Vespucci, recognised that it was a separate continent and gave it his name. The discovery unleashed events that were both terrible and far-reaching. They led to the diverse, dynamic and rapidly changing continent that is South America today.

A CONTINENT OF EXTREMES

The continent of South America stretches for 7,400 km from north to south and 5,150 km from east to west. It covers more than 17.8 million km², reaching far above the equator and dipping down to within 1,000 km of the Antarctic Circle. It is the fourth largest of the continents.

South America is a continent that defies imagination. The Andes, the longest mountain chain in the world, form a backbone along its western edge. More than fifty of the peaks are over 6,500 m high. The River Amazon easily beats records: its flow is equal to the next ten largest rivers in the world, and it drains an area twice the size of India.

A CONTINENT OF CONTRASTS

Above all, South America is a continent of contrasting peoples and cultures. It is a continent where peoples of European and African origin have mingled with indigenous (native) populations to produce vibrant communities; where religion influences much of daily life; and where football and music are part of the national identity.

The Amazon Basin contains the world's largest tropical rain forest. It covers nearly 7 million km², about 40 per cent of the continent's entire area. There are high plateaus, or tepuis, soaring thousands of metres vertically above the forest floor, which have never been explored. They formed the inspiration for Sir Arthur Conan Doyle's famous novel The Lost World, in which dinosaurs still roamed these tropical islands in the sky.

THE MAKING OF A CONTINENT

South America, as we know it, was formed between 150–200 million years ago when the super-continent known as Pangaea began to break up. South America was ripped away from Africa and began to drift slowly westwards, suspended on a layer of semi-molten rock, the earth's mantle. This huge continental plate came into contact with another, deeper, oceanic plate and was forced upwards, creating the vast mountain range of the Andes. The friction between the two plates caused rock to melt, producing a region of volcanic and earthquake activity, part of the 'Pacific ring of fire'.

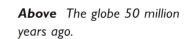

Above *The globe 50 million years ago.*

Left *This satellite view of the Earth shows both North and South America.*

THE GEOGRAPHY OF SOUTH AMERICA

The Andes mountain system is huge, extending over 6,400 km in length. In places it is over 800 km wide. The Andes contain the highest mountain peak outside Asia, Argentina's Cerro Aconcagua, which rises to 6,960 m. Here soars the giant condor, the world's largest vulture, now reduced to a few hundred birds. The Andes contain many volcanoes, and earthquakes can occur almost everywhere, often with disastrous consequences.

To the west of the Andes is a narrow coastal strip. Rivers forming in the Andes either drain west to the coast, or flow eastwards into the three great river basins of South America: the *llanos* (grassland) of Venezuela, drained by the Orinoco River; the Amazon Basin; and the Parana/Uruguay Basin that empties into the River Plate estuary.

The geography of South America is dramatic — it is dominated by the huge Andes mountain system, river basins and the highlands in the east.

QUAKE!

On Sunday 31 May, 1970 an earthquake, high in the mountains, set off a landslide in the Nevado region of Peru. Eighteen thousand people in the town of Yungay died. One survivor said, 'All gone, except some children – not mine – watching a circus and some old people lighting candles at the cemetery on the hill. When the avalanche came, a wind just blew people away. See that earth there? That is where my house and family are buried.'

Above *This view of the Andes Mountains was taken across Lake of the Horns in Patagonia, Argentina.*

Right *The Angel Falls in Venezuela are the highest in the world, plunging down nearly 1,000 m from the plateau of Auyaín Tepui, the Devil's Mountain.*

Much of the eastern 'bulge' of South America is made up of the Guiana Highlands and the Brazilian plateau, both made of hard rock much older than the Andes. The structure of these rocks has created sharp, sometimes vertically sided landforms, forming waterfalls of great height.

CLIMATE

The climate of South America is influenced by three main factors – latitude (its distance from the equator), altitude (how high it is above sea level) and the sea. Much of the continent is tropical or sub-tropical, but high altitudes in the west and east greatly reduce temperatures. The surrounding Pacific and Atlantic Oceans also influence the climate. Winds blowing off the sea bring over 2,500 mm of rain each year to parts of the east coast and the Pacific coast of Colombia and to southern Chile.

In contrast, no rainfall has ever been recorded at Calama, Chile, in the Atacama Desert. Here the massive, cold Humboldt current, sweeping along the northern coast of Chile, creates a block of cold air that prevents warmer, rain-bearing air from entering the region.

A fourth influence on the climate is human habitation, especially in urban regions where air pollution has increased temperatures and the amounts of rainfall.

Changing climates

There are seven different types of climate in South America. The Amazon basin and coasts influenced by onshore winds, have a tropical rainy climate. Rainfall is heavy throughout the year and daytime temperatures reach about 29 °C. Surrounding the Amazon basin is a tropical wet and dry region that receives six months of summer rain followed by six months of winter drought. Further to the north and south is a humid sub-tropical region that covers southern Brazil, Uruguay, Paraguay and north-eastern Argentina. Here temperatures are cooler and rainfall evenly distributed. Central and southern Argentina has a much drier (arid) climate, including the vast Patagonian desert.

The coast of Peru and northern Chile has an arid (dry) or semi-arid climate, mostly receiving less than 250 mm of rain and experiencing wide variations in temperature. Central Chile has a climate that is described as Mediterranean – meaning it is mild, with most of the rain falling during the winter. Further south, Chile experiences a temperate maritime climate, being cool, rainy and windy throughout the year. South America's mountain and upland regions experience wide variations in temperature and rainfall, depending on altitude.

SOUTH AMERICA'S CLIMATE ZONES

Tropical climates

Tropical rain forest

Savanna

Dry climates

Steppe

Desert

Mild climates

Marine west coast

Humid subtropical

Mediterranean

Cold climates

Tundra

VEGETATION

The areas of natural vegetation depend very much on the climate of the regions. Those regions receiving most rain are covered with tropical rain forest (*selva*). In southern Brazil and central and southern Chile, there is temperate or mixed forest, consisting of softwoods (conifers) as well as hardwoods. Tropical thorn forest covers much of north-eastern Brazil, western Paraguay and northern Argentina.

The tropical wet and dry regions are mostly covered by grasslands (*savanna*). Long dry winters prevent the growth of many types of trees. These areas have been used mostly for cattle ranching. Where conditions become cooler and dryer, prairie grassland (*pampas*) takes over. This in turn is replaced by thin scrub and then desert in arid regions. In central Chile there is an area of Mediterranean vegetation with evergreen trees and shrubs that are adapted to survive the dry summers. Mountainous regions have zones of vegetation depending on the altitude. These zones range from tropical crops (*tierra caliente*) to alpine meadows.

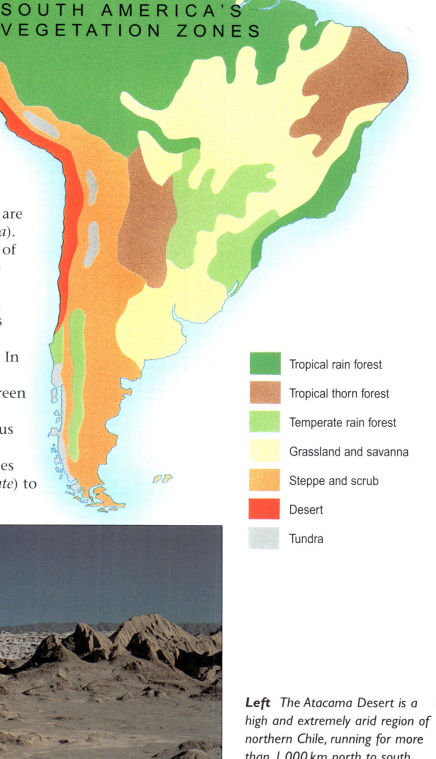

SOUTH AMERICA'S VEGETATION ZONES

- ■ Tropical rain forest
- ■ Tropical thorn forest
- ■ Temperate rain forest
- ■ Grassland and savanna
- ■ Steppe and scrub
- ■ Desert
- ■ Tundra

Left The Atacama Desert is a high and extremely arid region of northern Chile, running for more than 1,000 km north to south between the Andes and the Pacific coast.

THE HISTORY OF SOUTH AMERICA

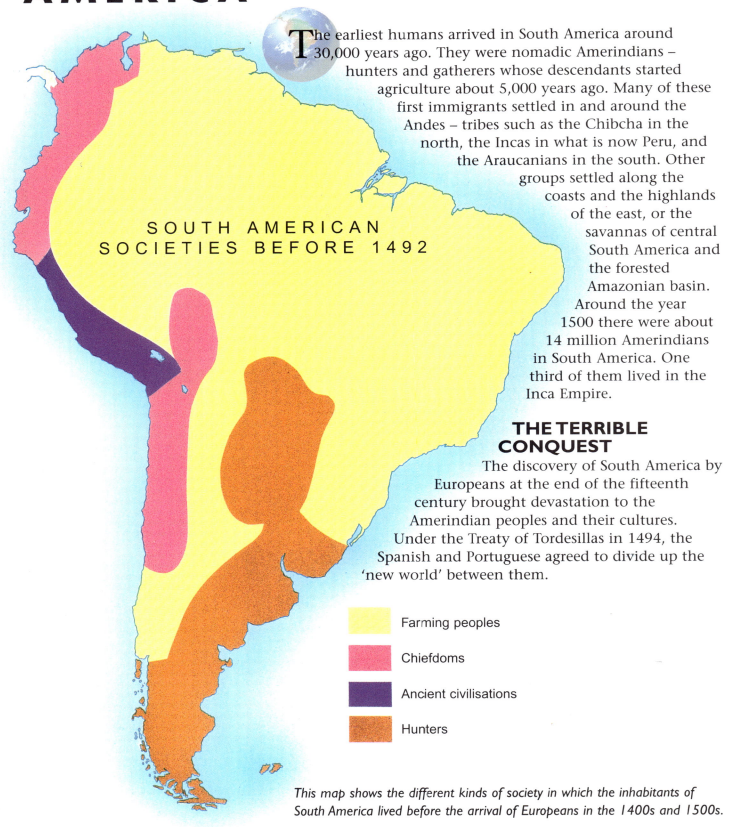

SOUTH AMERICAN SOCIETIES BEFORE 1492

The earliest humans arrived in South America around 30,000 years ago. They were nomadic Amerindians – hunters and gatherers whose descendants started agriculture about 5,000 years ago. Many of these first immigrants settled in and around the Andes – tribes such as the Chibcha in the north, the Incas in what is now Peru, and the Araucanians in the south. Other groups settled along the coasts and the highlands of the east, or the savannas of central South America and the forested Amazonian basin. Around the year 1500 there were about 14 million Amerindians in South America. One third of them lived in the Inca Empire.

THE TERRIBLE CONQUEST

The discovery of South America by Europeans at the end of the fifteenth century brought devastation to the Amerindian peoples and their cultures. Under the Treaty of Tordesillas in 1494, the Spanish and Portuguese agreed to divide up the 'new world' between them.

Farming peoples

Chiefdoms

Ancient civilisations

Hunters

This map shows the different kinds of society in which the inhabitants of South America lived before the arrival of Europeans in the 1400s and 1500s.

INCA CIVILIZATION

During the fourteenth and fifteenth centuries the Inca Empire expanded from central Chile to Ecuador. The Incas were a military people, but were also skilled farmers, using complex irrigation systems and terraced fields. Gold and silver were highly valued, and this was one of the reasons for the ruthless behaviour of the invading Spanish. The Inca Empire was a highly religious civilization. Temples and shrines were created for sun worship. Cuzco, seen here in ruins, was the capital of the great Inca Empire. The Sun Temple at Cuzco had a circumference of 350 m. Now only a few fragments of Inca culture remain among the Quechua-speaking peoples of Peru and Bolivia.

Right *The ruins of Winay Wayna, an Inca settlement on the terraced slope of a mountain.*

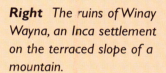

SOUTH AMERICA BY 1550

By the end of the sixteenth century, the Portuguese had driven deep into Brazil, while Spain dominated the surrounding countries. This is why Spanish is the common language of much of South America, and Portuguese is spoken in Brazil.

The continent was invaded by armies of conquistadors (conquerors) in search of land and gold. The most infamous of these was Francisco Pizarro, who conquered much of Peru between 1532 and 1534. The Spanish, with the advantage of horses and cannons, killed thousands of Incas and destroyed many of their cities and religious buildings. Huge quantities of gold and silver were shipped back to Europe.

Amerindians were forced to work in silver mines or on estates, gathering forest products such as vanilla, rubber and cocoa. Many died, and others caught European diseases such as influenza, to which they had no resistance. The survivors were organized into missions run by Christian orders, and adopted the new religion.

■ Area under Spanish control

■ Area under Portuguese control

AN EVOLVING SOCIETY

During the seventeenth century Britain, France and the Netherlands all gained footholds on the north-east coast. Much later, migrants from many other European countries settled in South America, attracted by the coffee plantations of southern Brazil and the rapidly growing cities of Uruguay, Argentina and Chile. In Colombia, Venezuela, Brazil and Peru, Europeans and native Amerindians inter-married to form large mixed populations called *mestizo* in Spanish South America and *mestico* in Brazil.

Apart from the Europeans, there was another important influence on South American culture. Because of labour shortages on the European-owned plantations, black Africans were brought to the continent as slaves. Today about 12 per cent of South America's population is of African origin. Most are still concentrated in the old plantation zones of north-eastern Brazil and along the Caribbean coast. Many have inter-married with white South Americans, forming a racial grouping known as the *mulatto*. Arab minorities also make an important contribution to the economy of most American countries.

Below South American society is the result of the interweaving of Amerindian, European and African traditions. But cultural differences between individual countries and groups remain, making South America an ethnically rich and varied continent.

Left *Early in the twentieth century, a quarter of a million Japanese entered South America, attracted by the opportunity of farming Brazil's open spaces. Here, a member of the Japanese community in Brazil watches World Cup football on the television.*

Below *These young people are being trained as members of The Shining Path, a group of guerrillas who followed the ideas of the Bolivian revolutionary hero, Che Guevara. He believed that revolutions should start in the countryside and then move to the cities.*

POWER STRUGGLES

It is only in recent years that most South American governments have returned from military rule to more democratic forms of leadership. Often the military regimes were brutal and oppressive. Secret police kept a state of fear. Groups who disagreed with the government were hunted down. Torture was common and many people simply disappeared, as happened in Argentina in the 1970s and 1980s. Bribery of officials was common. In 1992, the Brazilian president was dismissed for corruption.

Guerrillas

South America also has a history of violent attacks on its governments and people by terrorist or guerrilla groups. Sometimes these groups are a result of South America's drug trade; more often they are political groups of different beliefs or backgrounds, such as the extreme communist Shining Path group of Peru, whose leader Abimael Guzman was captured in a dramatic police trap in 1992. Another Peruvian guerrilla group calls itself *Tupac Amaru*, after an Inca king who led resistance to Spain.

A NEW DEMOCRACY

Many of South America's problems are rooted in its turbulent past. Harsh colonial rulers governed their territories with a rod of iron, and were only ousted from power by charismatic leaders behind whom the poor people could unite. Once the colonial period ended these leaders often became political bosses of their countries, establishing a link between military leadership (which had been necessary to win independence) and political power (which the military leaders took after independence was won).

This link between the military and politics continues today. Throughout the 1970s and 1980s, harsh right-wing Army generals often ran South American countries as their own personal properties. Foreign governments continued to give financial help to these régimes because they thought that it was preferable to communism, which they considered to be the alternative.

Now, though, the generals have been forced to give up power, as communism becomes a less powerful force. Elections take place in South America regularly, and people are able to exercise their democratic rights. However, the threat of the military interfering is always present.

Michel Camdessus, president of the International Monetary Fund (IMF). The IMF, together with the World Bank, lends money to countries in economic difficulty, but often imposes conditions that make life harder for the poorest people. Sometimes, the IMF's conditions also include an insistence on a stable, democratic government.

Left *Argentina's attempt to claim the Falkland Islands (called Islas Malvinas in Argentina) in 1982 led to a short war between Argentina and Britain. The war finished when British troops fought their way across the main island on foot and recaptured the capital, Port Stanley. Defeat led to the collapse of the military government in Argentina. The picture shows an Argentinian soldier in training.*

CASE STUDY

A visitor to Paraguay recently described these two contrasting scenes which, in many ways, show the continuing contrasts and conflicts that South America faces.

'Weeping and coughing, his longish, brown hair and dark suit drenched, Asunción's new mayor stands helpless as tear-gas canisters fly and fire engines spew jets of water along Calle Palma, the city's major shopping street. On this warm, spring day, bus drivers are striking in Paraguay's capital city. Protestors fill the street, shouting at

hundreds of police as they draw closer. But no one is taking orders from Carlos Filizzola, Asunción's first elected mayor in 454 years...

'This is still a place of innocence. It isn't just the setting of faded old buildings, brightly painted buses and wood floors and sputtering engines, dirt roads that snake towards hamlets lost in the green countryside. Paraguayans themselves seem to step from an earlier and simpler time.'

Source: *National Geographic*, Jan 1989: 'Cocaine's deadly reach'.

THE PEOPLES OF SOUTH AMERICA

RELIGION

Christianity is the major religion of South America, but it has mixed with other religions. Throughout the continent, there is a form of religion known as *candomblé* in Brazil and *santaria* in Spanish-speaking countries. This is really a mix of African beliefs and Roman Catholicism. In the countries of the Andes, such as Peru and Bolivia, gods similar to those of the Incas are worshipped in traditional ceremonies. Even older beliefs, in which the spirits of animals are called upon, also survive among the Amerindians.

LIVING TOGETHER

The intermingling of cultures sometimes causes conflict. In the Andean countries, tension can exist between the rich European city dwellers and the poorer Quechua and Aymará-speaking Amerindians living in surrounding rural communities.

KEEPING A CULTURE ALIVE

The peoples of the central Amazon basin, the Amerindians, are the most isolated from other cultures. Despite European settlement, invasion by gold miners and attempts to change their religion and way of life, Amerindian customs, languages and religions have survived. In towns and cities across the continent, streets are named after Amerindian groups and statues of past leaders dominate the squares. South American literature is full of Amerindian heroes, and their flute and drum music is now popular worldwide. With much international support, one group, the Yanomani, won their battle for a forest reserve three times the size of Belgium. But for the rest, particularly those in the cities, the battle to gain equal opportunities and keep their identity continues.

Right Once every year at the start of Lent, much of South America becomes a carnival. The continent explodes into colourful parades, music and dance. Although based around Roman Catholicism, these activities are really a mixture of different religions and politics. They may poke fun at a local landowner who treats peasant workers badly, a judge who favours the rich, or a priest who asks for money for his services.

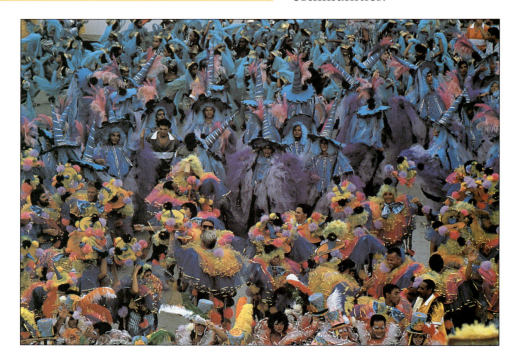

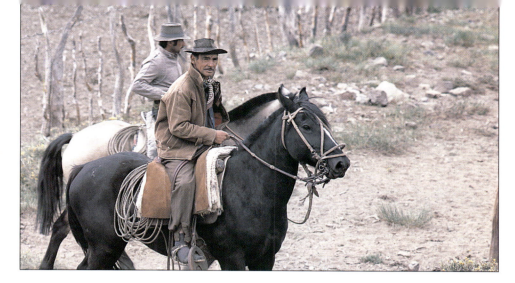

Right The opening of the grasslands to cattle during the nineteenth century resulted in a new type of South American, the gaucho or cowboy. Gauchos still work on the huge cattle ranches of Argentina, Uruguay, Venezuela and Brazil. They are mainly descended from Europeans, with some Amerindian influences.

Although racial discrimination is illegal throughout South America, people of African and Amerindian origin are limited to the margins of economic and political life. They earn less and die younger. Political groups such as the Union of Indigenous Peoples of Brazil, set up to campaign for Amerindian rights over land, may be one step towards a fairer future for the minorities.

Left These Quecha Amerindian women and children from Cotopaxi, Ecuador, are wearing traditional shawls. These brightly coloured shawls are very much part of South American culture — they are used to carry everything from babies to goods when going to the market.

GOOOOOAAAAAAALLLLLL!!!

Much of South America is football crazy. The game was introduced in about 1900 by British engineers. By the 1920s there were football leagues in Argentina, Brazil, Chile and Uruguay. South American teams have won the World Cup eight times. Rivalries between teams are intense. When a footballer scores a goal, the spectators go wild, while the match commentator makes the word go on for ever!

Right Here Diego Maradona combines powerful running with great skill to fend off a tackle from another player.

POPULATION

South America is the most urban of the developing continents. About 60 per cent of its population live in cities. Argentina, Uruguay and Chile are all close to 85 per cent urban. Over 17 million people live in the huge city of São Paulo in Brazil. Here there is a tremendous intermixing of cultures, while in rural areas it has been easier for different ethnic groups to remain separate. Many of these groups are Amerindians, but some are descended from European and African backgrounds.

A feature of South American society has been the move from the countryside to the cities. There is a great contrast between the well-off and well-educated, 'westernized' middle-class and the mass of poor people living in shanty towns (*favelas*) around the city margins. Life in these slums is often poor and short. Children – many homeless 'street children' – often roam the streets in gangs looking for opportunities, legal or illegal, to get money or food. Others scrape an existence from the disease-infested garbage mountains; waste from the other, richer city that they can see but which they can never enter.

However, the poor aren't helpless. Extended families and the work of churches provide support and community action.

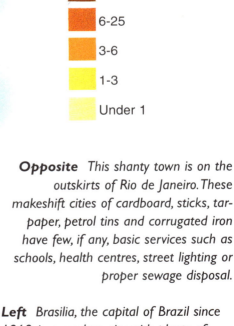

SOUTH AMERICA'S POPULATION DENSITIES

Inhabitants per km²

Over 100	
50-100	
25-50	
6-25	
3-6	
1-3	
Under 1	

Opposite This shanty town is on the outskirts of Rio de Janeiro. These makeshift cities of cardboard, sticks, tar-paper, petrol tins and corrugated iron have few, if any, basic services such as schools, health centres, street lighting or proper sewage disposal.

Left Brasilia, the capital of Brazil since 1960, is a modern city with plenty of open spaces. It was built 1,000 km inland from the other major cities of São Paulo and Rio de Janeiro, to encourage people to settle in the central region.

HUMAN DEVELOPMENT

Many South American countries provide a reasonable standard of living and education for their people. Argentina, Chile and Uruguay have literacy rates of over 90 per cent. Further down the scale is Bolivia, where over 35 per cent of the population are estimated to be illiterate. Amerindian groups tend to have lower literacy rates than other groups. The percentage of literate women is also generally less than that of men, while rural areas have a greater percentage of illiteracy than urban areas.

Differences between men and women extend to other areas of society. In general, women in South America have fewer opportunities than those in Europe or North America. They have little economic or political power, tend to marry earlier and have more children. The role of women is, to some extent, determined by religious and cultural values that go back many centuries. Many South American men still support the view that a woman's role should only be in the home.

HEALTHCARE

Healthcare and levels of nutrition in South America vary widely. In Bolivia, Ecuador, Peru, Guyana and Colombia many people don't have an adequate diet, in terms of both carbohydrate and protein intake. The leading causes of death are dysentery (in Colombia), tuberculosis (in Peru), whooping cough (in Bolivia, Ecuador and Peru) and measles (in Ecuador, Bolivia and Colombia).

MOTHER POWER

In one way at least, South American women have been able to use their position as mothers to powerful effect. During the late 1970s and early 1980s, Argentina's military government ruthlessly removed any young men it felt posed a danger to the regime. During this time, mothers at the Plaza de Mayo in Buenos Aires (shown below) joined together to protest at the disappearance of their sons. This challenge to the military rulers from mothers was hard to ignore. International publicity and support helped to secure the dismissal of the military regime.

Above Mothers with photos of their missing children.

Below This chart shows basic health, literacy and income data for most South American countries. Venezuela is technically the richest country because of its oil exports, but this wealth doesn't filter through to the average income. Also, Venezuela has introduced cut-backs since it has accumulated vast debts.

Country	Infant mortality per 1,000 births	Life expectancy men and women (years)	Adult literacy (% of population)	Average income ($)
Argentina	29	73	95	2780
Bolivia	100	56	63	650
Brazil	57	67	80	2920
Chile	–	73	90	2160
Colombia	37	69	88 (Indians 60)	1280
Ecuador	–	67	85	1020
Guyana	–	65	75	290
Paraguay	–	67	81	1210
Peru	76	65	80	1020
Surinam	–	70	65	3610
Uruguay	–	73	94	2560
Venezuela	33	70	86	2610

Source: *Philips Encyclopaedic World Atlas, 1993.*

Infant mortality rates are particularly high in some South American countries, despite improving medical facilities. In Bolivia 10 per cent of infants die before they reach the age of 1 year and life expectancy is about 56 years. In the wealthier countries, such as Argentina and Venezuela, life expectancy is more than 70 years.

Above In Bolivia, classes for adults are helping to improve the standard of literacy.

NETWORKS OF DEATH

One of the less attractive sides to South America's development is its involvement in the international drugs trade. Bolivia and Peru are the main cocaine-producing countries, while Colombia is the centre for refining and distribution. US agencies have estimated that the total sales value of cocaine (much of it on US streets) is $22 billion, equivalent to the GNP of a medium-sized country. Through fear and bribery, those who control drugs – the 'drug barons' – are able to influence the political and economic life of a country, even its legal system. Rival gang warfare, assassinations of judges and police officers, and bribery of state officials are common. When the Colombian government tried to crack down heavily on the drug gangs or cartels, they were met with such violence that thousands died. Bolivia and Peru are having more success by offering poor cocaine-producing farmers incentives (financial rewards) to grow alternative crops.

Right A soldier from an anti-narcotics (anti-drugs) unit sections off a field of heroin poppies before they are sprayed with glyphosate herbicides – chemicals which will destroy the crop in seven days. These units are constantly carrying out search and destroy operations against heroin and cocaine plantations.

A LAND OF RESOURCES

FOOD AND FARMING

Despite its growing industry, South America is still largely an agricultural continent. Soils in South America differ greatly in fertility. Those in tropical rainy areas are surprisingly infertile because most of their nutrients are washed away by the rain, or quickly broken down by bacteria and almost immediately taken up again by plants. In tropical forests, fertility is literally locked in the vegetation itself.

In more temperate areas, the dark-coloured soils of the grasslands are among the most fertile in the world. Grass decomposes to form a rich compost called humus. Countries such as Argentina and Uruguay contain vast areas of these rich, productive soils. Where South America's great rivers still regularly flood over, they leave a layer of mud, silt and sand over the surrounding land. This makes the soil very fertile.

Brazil has 300,000 km² of arable land (which is farmed for crops), 40 per cent of the continent's total. Argentina comes second, with 214,000 km². However, the lack of fertility of Brazil's tropical soils, and the low rainfall in much of Argentina, reduce their ability to grow crops. Even so, Brazil has long been the world's leading exporter of coffee and one of the leading producers of sugar cane and cacao (used to make chocolate).

- Wheat
- Maize
- Other cereals
- Cocoa, coffee, tea
- Fruit
- Forest
- ▼ Sugar cane
- Vines
- Cattle
- Sheep
- Pigs
- Fishing

Left Here, sugar cane is being cut in Brazil. The canes are crushed between heavy rollers to remove the sweet juice from which sugar is made.

Both Brazil and Argentina are major producers of beef cattle. Nearly 100 million cattle roam the pastures of Brazil, half that number in Argentina. The clearing of forests to make pasture for cattle has been a major cause of habitat destruction in Brazil.

Uruguay and Argentina are major producers of sheep for wool and meat. These sheep are being moved in Patagonia, the wild region at the tip of southern Argentina and Chile.

ECONOMY VERSUS ENVIRONMENT

The most important grain crops are maize, rice and wheat. Many South Americans also grow root crops such as cassava and potatoes. Food production overall in South America has increased in relation to population growth. However, crops are often sold for export, or go to feed cattle for overseas markets, rather than going to local people. Crops specifically grown for export (known as cash crops), such as bananas, coffee and sugar cane, may be grown in areas better suited to more local varieties. Such crops frequently need expensive fertilizers and pesticides that may damage fragile soils. These are not simple issues, because all countries depend on exports to buy the things they cannot produce themselves. Like other continents, South America has to balance the needs of its economy and people with the needs of the environment.

ABUNDANT FORESTS

South America has the largest area of tropical rain forest in the world. Tropical hardwoods are in demand worldwide. They are used in construction, furniture, household goods and musical instruments, even for coffins. Brazil is the second largest producer of timber in the world, although nearly 80 per cent of this is for fuel. Tropical forests are also a source of many other products such as quinine (a drug from the cinchona tree which is used to fight malaria), eucalyptol (a cough treatment), chicle (a base for chewing-gum), coconuts, rubber, tannin (used in the leather industry) and palm oil (for soap and cosmetics).

LABORATORIES IN THE SKY

Tropical rain forests have several distinct layers. The main canopy of trees spreads out at 25–30 m. Much taller, or emergent, trees grow out of the canopy to twice this height or more. Below the canopy are smaller trees and shrubs, depending on the amount of light getting through. Creepers and lianas wind their way up the trees and epiphytes – a group including orchids and ferns – grow high on the trees where they can reach the light.

In 1990 an international group of scientists developed a huge inflatable raft, carried by an airship, which could be placed gently on top of the canopy. The scientists in the raft could study the canopy's plants and animals through the netting in the raft's floor.

Below Forests support thousands of native Amerindian communities, many of whom live entirely off the natural products of the forest. These are Ashaninka people in the Peruvian Amazon.

FOOD FROM THE SEA

The oceans around South America are some of the most productive in the world. Off the coast of Peru the cold Humboldt current comes to the surface, bringing with it nutrients from the sea-bed. The nutrients encourage the growth of tiny floating plants (plankton), which provide food for animal plankton. These in turn fall prey to small fish, such as anchovy.

Peruvian fishermen catch anchovy in vast numbers. At one time, anchovy fishing made up 50 per cent of Peru's exports, but overfishing and changes in currents have reduced the number of anchovy dramatically. This has affected other fish such as tuna and sea bass, and the huge flocks of sea birds that circle overhead, like the Guanay cormorant. Now the droppings from these birds no longer enrich the water, and a once-thriving fishing industry is all but destroyed.

Fishing boats in Chimbote harbour, Peru. These boats fish for anchovy. The anchovy are ground into fishmeal for export as chicken feed and fertilizer.

MINERALS

South America is well supplied with mineral resources, but they are often poorly matched. For example, Brazil and Chile have huge deposits of iron ore but they haven't the type of coal needed to convert it from iron ore into steel. Brazil also has large stocks of manganese, platinum and bauxite, and Chile's copper reserves are the greatest in the world. Peru is another major producer of copper and iron, and Bolivia has long been among the world's leading tin exporters.

Other major mineral exports include lead, zinc, silver and mercury (Peru); gold and emeralds (Colombia); sulphur, iodine and nitrates (Chile); and phosphates (Brazil and Peru).

The extraction of these minerals can have disastrous effects on the environment. The mercury used by miners in Brazil to separate gold from river sediments pollutes the water. Sediment from mines near the coast settles over coral reefs and smothers them.

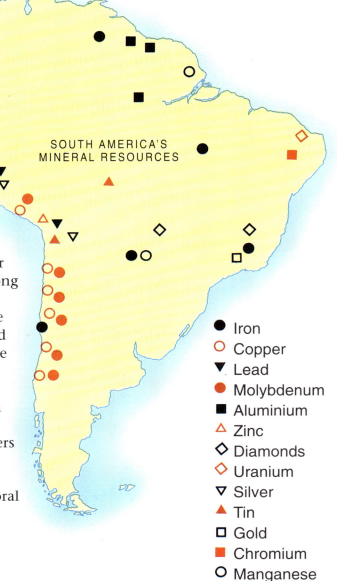

SOUTH AMERICA'S MINERAL RESOURCES

- ● Iron
- ○ Copper
- ▼ Lead
- ● Molybdenum
- ■ Aluminium
- △ Zinc
- ◇ Diamonds
- ◇ Uranium
- ▽ Silver
- ▲ Tin
- □ Gold
- ■ Chromium
- ○ Manganese

Below *An open-cast iron ore mine in Venezuela. Venezuela is a major exporter of iron ore.*

Above The Itaipú Dam on the River Parana, bordering Brazil and Paraguay, is the largest power complex on earth.

ENERGY

South America is both a major producer and consumer (user) of energy. Venezuela is the leading oil producer, followed by Ecuador, Bolivia and Peru. Colombia exports coal. In order to meet their rapidly growing energy needs, many South American countries are turning to hydroelectric power as their main source of energy. Over 75 per cent of South America's power production comes from this source. Rivers like the Amazon and Orinoco have great potential for hydroelectric power, but because of their distance from major urban and industrial areas their potential is limited.

Power from dams on the São Francisco River has brought about 1 million jobs to north-eastern Brazil. However, many of these jobs are in skilled, energy-intensive industries such as aluminium smelting, and do not always benefit the many unskilled workers in these areas.

Damming rivers to provide power can cause massive environmental damage. When land above the dam is flooded, forests are killed and local people have to move. Below the dam, water courses are altered and the regular flooding of river valleys interrupted, so that nutrients from the river no longer fertilize the land.

Below These workers are panning for gold at Cholo, near Quibdo in Colombia.

INDUSTRY

South America stands halfway between being a fully industrialized continent like North America and Europe, and a developing one like Africa. Venezuela has the third-highest Gross National Product (GNP) of the South American countries, although much of this is based on its enormous oil exports. Income in the country itself is very unevenly distributed. Because of its huge size, Brazil has the greatest GNP overall (US$ 472 billion), with Argentina second (US$ 244 billion). Guyana (US$ 285 million) has the lowest level of production.

BRAZIL

IMPORTS
- Raw materials 37.7%
- Other
- Fuels & lubricants 20.5%
- Capital goods 26.5%

EXPORTS
- Other
- Coffee 5.2%
- Chemical products 6.3%
- Metallic ores 7.1%
- Soya beans 10.6%
- Metallurgical products 17.7%
- Transport equipment 11.4%

ECUADOR

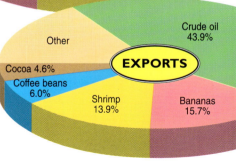

IMPORTS
- Inputs for industry 45.1%
- Other
- Non-durable consumer goods 7.4%
- Transport equipment 11.1%
- Capital goods for industry 20.9%

EXPORTS
- Crude oil 43.9%
- Other
- Cocoa 4.6%
- Coffee beans 6.0%
- Shrimp 13.9%
- Bananas 15.7%

VENEZUELA

IMPORTS
- Raw materials 41.4%
- Other
- Construction materials 3.0%
- Transport materials 14.6%
- Machinery & equipment 26.9%

EXPORTS
- Crude oil & derivatives 79.7%
- Other
- Aluminium 6.6%

TRADE

South America's main exports are related to its agriculture and raw materials rather than to manufacture. After oil, the leading exports are coffee, iron ore, soybeans, copper, beef, maize, bananas, cacao and cotton. However, manufacturing is becoming more important in most South American countries as they become increasingly industrialized. Brazil is now a major manufacturing nation. Machinery and other metal products, and transport equipment, make up its most important exports. Peru is also an important manufacturing nation. Over 30 per cent of Chile's exports are now made up of industrial products, while over 20 per cent of Argentina's GDP is based on its manufacturing industry alone.

Traditionally, most of South America's trade has been with countries outside the continent. The USA is the leading trade partner for both imports and exports, followed by Europe.

In an attempt to become less dependent on outside trade, most of the South American countries joined together to form an internal trading alliance, the *Asociación Latinoamericana de Integración* (*Aladi*) in 1980. Even so, trade between South American countries still only forms 15 per cent of total imports and exports. Now countries are moving towards more specific trading and customs agreements with each other, which will reduce their reliance on US and European markets even further.

Above *Coffee is one of South America's most important exports. Here beans are being spread out to dry in Brazil.*

Left *Apart from many companies which make parts for international industries, Brazil also manufactures its own products for internal sale and for export. This picture shows the inside of one of the country's car factories.*

TRANSPORT

Not surprisingly, the most industrialized countries have the most highly-developed transport networks. Argentina, Brazil and Chile have by far the longest rail networks; they also have the most highways and gravel road systems. Argentina has 406,200 km of railways, which are state owned, but are actually losing money. There are 219,200 km of roads, although less than 20 per cent are surfaced. Brazil has five times this figure. Guyana, on the other hand, has no public railways and the few roads are confined to coastal areas.

All the larger countries have major international airports. Chile, for example, is served by over twenty international airlines. However, domestic or internal flights are just as important to the economy of South America, especially in countries with few roads or mountainous terrain. The Andes make transport over land difficult in countries like Colombia, so there are daily flights between Bogotá and the principal towns.

Below In addition to rail and highways, Brazil, Argentina, Venezuela and Colombia have extensive inland waterways. Brazil, for example, has 35,100 km of navigable rivers and canals, that is rivers and canals that are wide, deep and safe enough to be sailed through.

RUNNING ON ALCOHOL

In order to become less dependent on oil, Brazil launched a programme to distil alcohol (ethanol) from sugar cane. By 1985, 85 per cent of new cars sold were run on alcohol. In 1990, there were 4.5 million alcohol-driven cars on Brazil's roads. Although producing less energy than petrol, alcohol also produces very little pollution.

However, as the price of oil dropped and government support for the programme diminished, there has been a gradual drift back to petrol-driven cars. But there is also a programme to find a substitute for diesel, using sunflower seed oil, palm oil or soya. The day of the vegetable-driven car is not yet over!

Ordinary petrol and alcohol (alcool) on sale side by side in Recife, Brazil.

THE PROBLEM OF DEBT

One of South America's most important problems is its enormous foreign debt – that is, the amount of money it owes to other countries. Although this debt is partly due to individual countries buying more goods than they sell abroad (trade imbalance), there are many other reasons. For example, many South American countries suffer from high rates of inflation, which damages trade. Like many other countries, they have also gone through a period of recession that has affected their ability to produce goods.

During the 1970s and 1980s, when oil prices were high and the world economy seemed to be expanding, international banks were eager to give massive loans to South American countries to help their development. The banks expected to be repaid with high rates of interest.

Below *Loans from the World Bank financed huge dams and ambitious highway schemes. This is the Pan American Highway across the Nazca Desert in Peru.*

TWO VIEWS OF ECONOMIC DEVELOPMENT IN ARGENTINA

'My father was a travelling salesman and I worked side by side with him, helping him from door to door. And when he was able to open a small store, he sent me out to the stores of competitors to look at prices. If sugar was priced at 20 cents a pound, he would sell it for 18.'
– **Carlos Menem, President of Argentina, 1995**

'I never believed that I, or my son, would see the changes being made now. All my life I have seen the country go only down, down, down.'– Argentine businessman on Argentina's economic recovery, 1994

This graph compares the debts in US$ billions of some South American countries.

Brazil	111
Argentina	64
Venezuela	33
Chile	18
Peru	17.5
Colombia	16.7
Ecuador	10.1
Uruguay	4.7
Bolivia	4.5
Paraguay	3.5
Guyana	3
Surinam	1

The predicted expansion did not last, however. The countries had to focus all their efforts on repaying the interest on the loans, rather than on their own development. The banks and other international organizations tried to find ways of reducing the debts. For example, some debts were simply written off or 'sold' on to other buyers at huge reductions. Countries owing money (debtor countries) could 'buy back' their debts, again at greatly reduced rates. Some debts were taken on by companies in exchange for shares in local businesses.

In some of the most recent and imaginative schemes, the value of debts is exchanged for agreements to carry out conservation projects in the debtor countries. Both Brazil and Bolivia have been involved in these so-called 'debts for nature' agreements.

Even so, the problem of debt remains the major obstacle to recovery in many South American countries. The continent's increasing reliance on its own, rather than outside, resources may be the first step in breaking the chain of debt, and the poverty that comes from it.

Below *Despite the continent's debts, progress is still being made. The completion of a 700 km section of railway between Columbia, Brazil and Santa Cruz, Bolivia, – the Trans-continental Line – means that the Chilean port of Arica on the Pacific coast is now linked with Rio de Janiero on the Atlantic coast.*

THE ENVIRONMENT

The Amazon Basin contains the world's largest and ecologically most important tropical rain forest. A 1000 hectare patch of forest contains over 3 thousand different species of plants and animals. They include the anaconda, the world's largest snake (capable of swallowing a goat whole); the strange pig-like tapir; and tree-climbing anteaters. There are too many different species of insect to count and many haven't even been named yet. The Amazonian rain forest is so huge, it creates its own climate, regulating rainfall and temperature, controlling the flow of water and possibly affecting the oxygen and carbon dioxide balance of the earth's atmosphere.

The Amazonian rain forest is currently being destroyed at a rate of between 1.5 per cent and 4 per cent every year. Accurate figures are hard to find because much of the destruction is illegal or unrecorded. Trees are cut down mainly for timber, fuel and to make space for farming. Huge forest fires, often caused deliberately, cause further damage. As the trees are lost, the thin, exposed soils are washed away by the torrential rains. Just one storm can remove 185 tonnes of soil from a single cleared hectare. After the rain, the sun bakes the earth hard so that it is often unable to support any kind of vegetation.

MANAGING THE RAIN FOREST

Research has shown that traditional, non-destructive uses of the rain forest (for example tapping rubber, harvesting fruit, oils and medicinal plants, and practising agro-forestry) is far more economic than logging, 'slash and burn' agriculture or ranching. In Peru, Yanesha Amerindians are now managing their forests by cutting trees in narrow strips, leaving wide sections of forest intact to eventually grow back over the felled areas. Brazil itself slowed down the destruction by no longer encouraging logging companies with extra payments, clamping down on illegal felling, establishing reserves and improving logging techniques.

Below The construction of the Belem-Brasilia Highway in the 1960s opened up the Amazon rain forest for logging and 'slash and burn' clearance for agriculture.

THE CYCLE OF DESTRUCTION

Some of the most badly affected areas are the Brazilian states of Mato Grosso, Rondonia, Acre and southern Para. Until 1960, Rondonia was inhabited only by Amerindians and rubber tappers. By the late 1970s, 5 thousand people were arriving each month. Many of them moved there from southern Brazil as part of a government scheme. Indigenous tribes came into conflict with the new arrivals or were driven off their land by the powerful logging and mining companies.

The newly cleared land yielded only one or two annual crops before the soil began to lose its fertility. New areas were opened up, but these too quickly became exhausted. Between 1975 and 1980, deforestation in Rondonia increased at a rate of 37 per cent each year.

Unable to support crops, the land was sold to wealthy landowners for ranching. Soon the settlers, with no land and little money, returned to the shanty towns on the outskirts of the cities.

Below One study showed that fruit and latex from tropical forests were worth nine times as much as the timber. Here, Amazonian rubber is being used to make gloves.

These are annual losses of tropical forests in South America

- More than 400,000 hectares
- Between 40,000 and 400,000 hectares
- Less than 40,000 hectares

HABITATS UNDER THREAT

Brazil's Atlantic forest on the east coast is now only 1 per cent of its size in Columbus's time. First exploited for the braza tree that gave the country its name, the fertile land was then cleared for sugar cane. The discovery of gold and diamonds led to an invasion of prospectors. As the mines were exhausted, the miners turned to farming, clearing more land for coffee, banana and rubber plantations and setting fire to the forest to drive out the Amerindians. Towns and then cities such as Rio de Janeiro and São Paulo grew up.

The fragments of forest that remain still manage to contain two-thirds of Brazil's butterfly species. But the woolly spider monkey – Brazil's largest primate – has been reduced from 400,000 to 400; the golden lion tamarin is down to a few hundred; the maned sloth to just a few. The tradition of shooting small birds, or keeping them as caged pets, has endangered many songbird species. National parks and reserves cover less than a tenth of what remains of this forest.

The Andean condor once flew throughout the Andes; now it is usually only found in Peru and Argentina. Between 1989–1991, 22 condors, reared in captivity, were released into three protected areas on the Colombian Andes. Each condor was fitted with a radio tracking device so its progress could be monitored. Four years later, at least 75 per cent had survived.

Left The largest common herbivore of the grasslands is the capybara, a giant, semi-aquatic rodent (related to rats and mice), that can weigh up to 80 kg and is bred on ranches for its meat.

ROLLING GRASSLANDS

South America's grasslands range from the wet tropical *llanos* of Venezuela and Colombia to the drier, rolling *pampas* of Argentina. Compared to the forests they have few species, but they are no less important. The jaguar, ocelot and cougar are the main predators, along with the maned wolf and bush dog. The best-known bird is the rhea, a giant, flightless inhabitant of the *pampas*. South American grasslands haven't the huge herds of antelope and zebra that cover the *savannas* of central Africa. These areas are not as threatened as the tropical forests, but overgrazing is beginning to wear out large areas of *pampas*.

DON'T BREATHE THE AIR!

A haze of smog, caused by the reaction of sunlight on pollutants from car exhausts and industry, often hangs all day over cities like Caracas, São Paulo and Rio de Janeiro. In an attempt to improve Santiago's air quality, the Chilean authorities ban a fifth of all cars from the roads each day. Brazil has introduced heavy fines and closed factories to clean up Cubatão, near São Paulo – known as the 'Valley of Death'. But progress is slow and it costs money that most countries can hardly afford. Meanwhile the poor, often forced to live where pollution is worst, suffer the most.

Below A haze of smog hangs over São Paulo on a clear winter's day

SOUTH AMERICA IN THE WORLD TODAY

South America is standing at a crossroads. With much of its huge resource of raw materials unused, and with its dynamic peoples not yet over-burdened by population pressures, it is ready to become the new industrialized powerhouse of the world. But it has not yet become so. Crippling debts and, until recently, governments hampered by corruption or oppressive regimes, have held back development.

We are beginning to see a new South America emerge. One that is increasingly dependent on its own massive resources rather than on the influence and finance of other continents, like North America and Europe. The new South America is developing as a major economic and industrial power that will rival and possibly overtake the economies of more so-called developed countries. But South America is also a continent in which terrible poverty, hunger and disease still dominate the lives of millions of people; where many are still denied human rights; and where environmental problems continue to grow.

Above *Groups of indigenous peoples meet at the Global Forum, a meeting for non-government organizations (NGOs), close to the Earth Summit. Threats to the way of life of such peoples was a major theme at the Forum.*

Left *People displaced by the construction of the Tucuruí dam in Brazil demonstrate that the land they have been offered cannot replace the homes they were forced to leave.*

A SUSTAINABLE CONTINENT?

In June 1992, world leaders from over one hundred and fifty countries met in Rio de Janeiro to discuss the state of the world's environment and its people. The meeting was called the Earth Summit. Although its recommendations were complex, its basic message was simple: that present generations must be able to meet their needs without damaging the earth's ability to support future generations.

In the past in South America, massive loans from major institutions like the World Bank, encouraged projects that were unsustainable. For example, huge dams and highway schemes brought some benefits but often did more damage and harmed more people than they helped. If South America is to develop successfully into a more industrialized continent, it must safeguard the basic resources on which it depends.

A huge crowd outside the São Paulo Business Centre watches the 1994 World Cup Final on a giant screen. (Brazil beat Italy on penalties after the teams had played extra time.)

A CONTINENT FIT FOR THE FUTURE

South America also has to face the challenge of the widening gap between rich and poor, its record on human rights, and the future of its indigenous people. Although there have been improvements in education and healthcare, economic pressures have slowed these improvements in recent years. Often governments provide expensive modern health services rather than basic healthcare for all. South America is faced with a series of choices about how it should develop in the future. In making those choices, it must take into account the needs and hopes and identities of its many different peoples.

TIMELINE

BC **30,000** Arrival of original (Amerindian) inhabitants.

5000 Hunter-gatherers began to settle and take up agriculture.

3200 Pottery in use in Ecuador and Colombia.

2000 First evidence of metal-working in Peru; use of pottery spreads among farmers.

1800–1900 People settle in permanent villages in Peru; evidence of religious organization, including temples.

900-200 Chavin culture flourishes in Peru, producing work in gold and silver.

200 Paracus Necropolis culture in Peru; producing brilliantly coloured, embroidered textiles.

AD **200–600** Regional development and experiments in technology (pottery and engineering) among the Mochica people of the north coast and the Nazca people of the south coast of Peru.

400 Incas begin to establish themselves on the Pacific coast.

600–1000 Local cultures merge under two great city empires, Tiahuanaco in Bolivia and Huari in Peru, which spread religion over a wide area.

1000–1483 Decline of the Tiahuanaco and Huari empires and the re-emergence of local cultures and towns. The Chimu peoples build large towns on the north coast of Peru. Ancestors of the Incas gather around Cuzco, in Peru.

1200–1300 Beginning of early Inca period in Peru. The leader, Mano Capac, makes Cuzco his capital and begins to make small invasions.

1438 The late Inca period when the emperor, Pachacuti Inca, begins to conquer the surrounding kingdoms.

1470 Incas conquer the Chimu kingdom.

1493–1525 Reign of Emperor Huayna Capac, the greatest Inca conqueror. He founds a second capital at Quito, Ecuador.

1494 Treaty of Tordesillas. Pope Alexander VI decides on the splitting of the 'New World' into Spanish and Portuguese empires.

1500–1502 Amerigo Vespucci explores the South American coast.

1504 Vespucci publishes an account of his voyages to South America.

1507 The New World is named America after its European discoverer.

1510 First African slaves are brought to South America.

1521–1549 The Spanish colonize Venezuela.

1530 The Portuguese begin to colonize Brazil.

1532–1534 Francisco Pizarro conquers much of the Inca Empire.

1572 Topa Amaru, the last Inca ruler, is captured and executed. Francis Drake, an English captain, begins attacking Spanish American harbours.

1608 The state of Paraguay is founded by the Jesuits.

1766 Britain occupies the Falkland Islands.

1803 Britain obtains British Guiana from the Dutch.

1803 Britain obtains British Guiana.

1808–1830 Wars of independence from Spanish and Portuguese colonial rule. Formation of most of the modern states of South America, including Argentina, Paraguay, Venezuela, Colombia, Uruguay and Chile.

1822 Brazil declares independence.

1833 Britain claims the Falkland Islands.

1864–1870 Paraguay fights a war with neighbouring countries. The population is reduced by half.

1879 Wars between Chile, Bolivia and Peru.

1889 Brazil becomes a republic after the king is deposed.

1903 Panama establishes independence from Colombia and gains the protection of the USA.

1917 South American states join the USA and other European countries in the war with Germany.

1932–1935 Wars between Paraguay and Bolivia over disputed territory.

1938 Unsuccesful Nazi (fascist Germany) plots to undermine governments in Chile and Brazil.

1942 Brazil declares war on Germany and Japan; all other states, except Argentina, cut off diplomatic relations with Germany and Japan.

1943 A revolution in Argentina brings Colonel Juan Peron to power as military ruler.

1946 Juan Peron becomes President of Argentina.

1955 President Peron is overthrown during a revolution.

1960 Brasilia becomes the new capital of Brazil.

1965–1980 Many South American countries come under rule by military dictatorships.

1966 British Guiana becomes independent.

1967 Che Guevara, the leader of the guerrilla movement against the military dictatorship in Bolivia, killed.

1970 Massive earthquake and landslip in Peru kills 60,000 people. Guyana becomes a republic.

1973 Revolution in Chile, supported by the USA, overthrows the Communist government. Juan Peron becomes President of Argentina again, but dies within a year.

1975 Surinam gains independence from Holland.

1976 The 'dirty war' in Argentina. Government opponents 'disappear' (are murdered or imprisoned and tortured by the regime).

1982 Argentina invades the Falkland Islands; Britain sends a naval taskforce and retakes the islands.

1982–1990 Democratic governments restored to most of South America.

1985 Volcanic eruption in Colombia buries four towns in ash, rocks and water, killing over 20,000 people. Ex-president Videla of Argentina jailed for life for violations of human rights.

1986 Argentina wins the World Cup.

1988 Chilean dictator, General Pinochet, defeated in elections and his cabinet resigns.

1989 Carlos Menem wins the presidential elections in Argentina.

1992 Brazilian president, Fernando Collar de Mello is accused of corruption. Terrorist leader of the Shining Path movement, Abimael Guzman, arrested in Lima, Peru. President Carlos Perez of Venezuela survives an attempt by the military to overthrow him.

1993 Douglas Hurd becomes the first British Cabinet Minister to visit Argentina since the Falklands War. The drugs 'baron' Pablo Escobar is killed in Colombia. Brazil votes not to restore the monarchy.

1994 The Bolivian government announces new measures to regulate coca (cocaine) production. The Colombian football star Andres Escobar is murdered after scoring an 'own goal' during the World Cup. Violent crime rises in Venezuela following tough economic measures – 3,408 people are killed in 9 months, strikes and water shortages occur, government takes over most Venezuelan banks.

1995 Princess Diana of Britain visits Argentina on a goodwill mission.

GLOSSARY

Administration How a country or organization is run.

Agro-forestry 'Underplanting' of crops in forested areas; allows food to be grown and fruit or other harvest from the trees to be obtained at the same time.

Alluvial Describes soil formed as a result of the flooding of rivers.

Altitude Elevation or height above sea level.

Arable Farming where crops are grown.

Biodiversity Variety of animals and plants; high biodiversity is usually a sign of a healthy environment.

Cash crops Crops grown specifically for export to generate income for a country.

Commodity Any article or product that can be traded.

Constitution Basic set of principles by which a country is governed.

Coup An attempt by a military or political group to take power by force.

Culture Aspects of a country or society that make it distinctive – its way of life, art, music, religion.

Distil To separate two or more substances, usually by heating, in order to purify or make more concentrated.

Ecology All the factors that relate to the type of plants and animals found in a particular area and their relationship to each other.

Economy The system of production of goods and services; distribution of income, exchange with other countries and consumption.

Eco-tourism Tourism based on a country's wildlife resources, can persuade local people to conserve, rather than exploit, wildlife and its habitats.

Energy-intensive Using a lot of energy.

Foreign debt How much a country owes other countries or international banks.

Free market Economic system in which trade and commerce are not restricted or controlled by government.

Guerrilla Person involved in warfare against an established government, usually in support of a cause.

Habitat A specific set of conditions in which plants and animals live, eg. rain forest or grassland.

Human rights Basic rights, eg. freedom of speech,which should be available to everyone.

Humus Organic part of soil, formed by decomposition of plants.

Hydroelectricity Electricity produced by water power, usually by damming a river.

Interest on loans Additional payment due when an individual or a country borrows money from a bank or other lending institution.

Junta A military political group that has taken power by force and which usually rules in an oppressive way.

Latex Sap of the rubber tree, collected for use in rubber production without damaging the tree.

Mantle of the earth A semi-molten, rocky layer beneath the earth's crust.

Migrants People moving into an area from another area, often under pressure of poverty or homelessness.

Natural selection Process by which animals and plants adapt and evolve into different species over a period of time.

Nutrients Dissolved chemicals such as nitrates and phosphates that promote plant growth.

Oppression System of control or government over people that reduces their human rights.

Privatization Selling off of state-owned industry to private investment (private ownership).

Recession Period during which a country's economy is in decline.

Slash and burn A system of farming in which land is cleared of vegetation which is then burnt. This system soon results in poor soil.

Subsidy Payment, usually by government, to support a particular activity, eg. farming or forestry.

Subsistence When people grow crops to support themselves rather than selling for profit.

Terrorism Imposing political will or views on a country by violent means.

Urbanized Where a large proportion of the population is concentrated in towns and cities.

FURTHER INFORMATION

BOOKS FOR CHILDREN

Brazil (Economically Developing Countries series, Wayland, 1996)

Mexico (Economically Developing Countries series, Wayland, 1996)

Brazil (Country Fact Files series, Macdonald Young Books, 1996)

Mexico (Country Fact Files series, Macdonald Young Books, 1996)

Mexico (On the Map series, Macdonald Young Books)

The Amazon (The World's Rivers series, Wayland, 1992)

The Amazon Rainforest and Its People (People and Places series, Wayland, 1993)

REFERENCE/ADULT BOOKS

Chronicle of the 20th Century, J L International Publications, 1994.

Collins Atlas of World History, Collins, 1987.

The Economist Book of Vital World Statistics, The Economist (latest edition).

The Economist World Atlas, The Economist, 1992.

The Guiness Guide to People and Cultures, Guiness Publishing, 1992.

Philips Encyclopaedic World Atlas, George Philips, 1993.

Philips Geographical Digest 1996–97 Heinemann Educational, 1996

Times Atlas of World History, Times Publishers, 1993.

Usborne Illustrated Guide To World History Dates, Jane Chisholm, Usborne Publishing, 1987.

The World Atlas of Exploration, Eric Newby, Mitchell Beazley, 1975.

The Cambridge Encyclopedia of Latin America, Cambridge University Press, 1992.

In addition there are many encyclopaedias and CD Roms that have up-to-date information about developments in South American countries. For example, Whitakers Almanac, published each year by Whitaker and Sons, has a gazetteer on every country in the world.

There are also a number of articles about South America in periodicals such as *National Geographic*, which have stunning photography. These give a valuable insight into the people and culture of the continent.

INDEX

Numbers in **bold** refer to illustrations and photographs.